Insects
Primary

Save time and energy planning thematic units with this comprehensive resource. We've searched through the 1989–1999 issues of **The MAILBOX**® and **Teacher's Helper**® magazines to find the best ideas for you to use when teaching a thematic unit on insects. Included in this book are favorite units from the magazines, single ideas to extend a unit, and a variety of reproducible activities. Pick and choose from these activities to develop your own complete unit or to simply enhance your current lesson plans. You're sure to find everything you need right here in this book to create an integrated unit that will give your youngsters something to buzz about!

Editors:
Karen A. Brudnak
Kimberly Fields
Sharon Murphy

Artists:
Cathy Spangler Bruce
Kimberly Richard

Cover Artist:
Kimberly Richard

www.themailbox.com

©1999 by THE EDUCATION CENTER, INC.
All rights reserved.
ISBN# 1-56234-327-0

Manufactured in the United States
10 9 8 7 6 5 4 3 2

Table Of Contents

Thematic Units

More Creepy, Crawly Ideas.... 22

Look in this section for bulletin-board ideas, art projects, math activities, and a variety of other insect-related ideas. This selection of activities will provide your budding entomologists with a swarm of learning opportunities!

Reproducible Activities

Thematic Units...

from The MAILBOX® magazine.

Much Ado About BUGS!

Feeling a little squeamish about exploring the sometimes creepy, sometimes crawly world of bugs? Put your worries aside. This collection of activities is swarming with fascinating facts and enticing activities your students are sure to love. So when you're ready to get the dirt on bugs—dig in!

ideas by Michele Converse Baerns and Jill Hamilton

A Buggy Beginning

Bugs are really amazing animals! To begin your bug unit, enlarge each of the six bug patterns on page 9 onto a 12" x 18" sheet of construction paper. Trim around each shape; then cut each shape into four or five large puzzle pieces. Divide students into six groups and give each group a set of puzzle pieces to assemble. After a group has constructed its puzzle and identified the resulting bug, give the group a book that contains information about its bug and some colorful markers. Challenge the group to label the back of each piece of its puzzle with a different fact about its bug. Set aside time for the groups to share their completed projects. If desired, laminate the completed puzzles and place each puzzle in a large resealable plastic bag. Store the puzzle bags at a center for further hands-on exploration!

What Is An Insect?

Share these ten fascinating facts about insects with your students:

- Insects are small animals with six legs. Insects use their legs to run, walk, jump, dig, and even sing!
- There are approximately five million different kinds of insects in the world.
- Insects wear their skeletons on the outside of their bodies. This *exoskeleton* protects an insect's body like a suit of armor.
- An insect has a heart, a brain, a tummy, air sacs, and nerves. These organs don't look like human organs, but they function in similar ways.
- All insects are cold-blooded. Sometimes big bugs shiver before they fly. What they are really doing is warming up their flight muscles so they'll work!
- Most insects live short lives. Some adult insects only live a few hours!
- Insects do not have noses; they smell with their antennae, or feelers.
- Insects can see, smell, and hear some things that humans cannot.
- Scientists are not sure what insects can feel.
- Insects communicate with each other in a variety of ways. Some insects flash lights, sing, dance, or use smelly chemicals to signal each other.

The Insect Issue

Even though insects—the largest animal group—are often very beneficial to humans, they are not very popular. Take a class poll before you continue your study of insects to find out if your youngsters are in favor of saving or stomping out the insect population. Record the outcome of the class poll; then have students vote again at the completion of the unit. Have students compare the outcomes of the two polls and comment on any changes of opinion.

An Insect's Body

The body of an insect has three sections. The *head*—where eyes, antennae (feelers), and jaws are found; the *thorax*—where legs and wings are attached; and the *abdomen*—where food is digested and eggs are produced. To reinforce the body parts of an insect, have each student make a marshmallow bug. To make the edible bug, use peanut butter to join three large marshmallows—the head, thorax, and abdomen. Poke six pretzel-stick legs into the thorax and two shoestring-licorice feelers into the head. Use peanut butter to attach two mini chocolate-chip eyes to the head and a pair of potato-chip wings (or wing shapes cut from Fruit Roll-Ups®) to the thorax. There you have it, a bug that's good enough to eat!

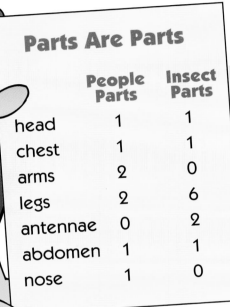

Parts Are Parts

	People Parts	Insect Parts
head	1	1
chest	1	1
arms	2	0
legs	2	6
antennae	0	2
abdomen	1	1
nose	1	0

Us And Them

Even though humans are very different from insects, they have several similarities. Enlist your students' help in creating a chart like the one shown; then complete the chart under your students' direction. After discussing the similarities and differences that humans and bugs share, use the chart as a springboard for a bug-related math lesson. Pose questions like "If two insects are in a room all alone, how many legs are in the room?" and "If you're counting noses, how many would you count on three people and three insects?" Student interest in math is sure to soar!

Checking Out Bugs

One of the best ways to learn about bugs is to watch them! For this activity each child needs a nine-ounce plastic drink cup, an eight-inch section of nude-colored panty hose that is knotted at one end, and a wooden craft stick. Have each student slide the section of hose onto her cup as shown, then set the craft stick inside the resulting bug observatory.

Take your students outdoors and ask each child to put several blades of grass, a small rock, and a piece of twig in her bug observatory. Then instruct each student to remove her craft stick and search for a bug. (The craft stick can be used to scoop the bug into its temporary home.) Once a student places a bug in her observatory, she slides the panty-hose covering over the top of her cup to prevent the bug's escape. Back in the classroom, distribute copies of page 10 and give each child (or group of children) a hand lens. Ask the students to complete the activity as they observe the bugs they've collected. As soon as everyone has completed the activity, take the students back outdoors so they may return the bugs to their natural habitats. Plan to repeat this activity several times during your study of bugs.

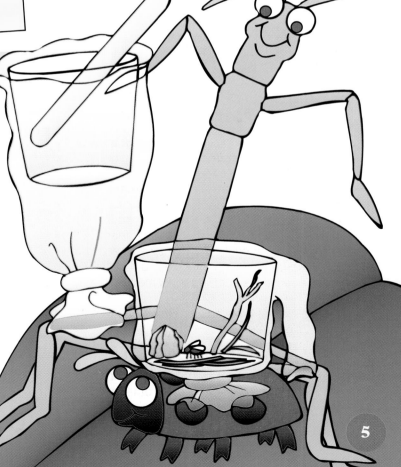

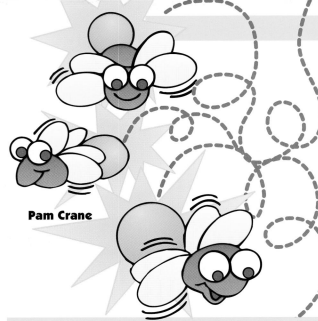

Pam Crane

Figuring With Fireflies

On a summer night, a field of fireflies is a sight to behold! These amazing insects—which are actually beetles, not flies—make a bright greenish light that can be seen at night. *Ten Flashing Fireflies* by Philemon Sturges (North-South Books, 1995) is a fun way to introduce students to these amazing critters. Hidden in the repetitive language of the story are simple addition and subtraction concepts. Plan to read the story more than once. Then during your second or third reading, have volunteers write number sentences on the chalkboard that represent the firefly activity shown in the book's illustrations. Discuss the number patterns that are observed. Later display the book at a center along with a supply of bookmaking materials. No doubt several of your enthusiastic entomologists will be interested in creating variations of this unique bug book.

Ladybug! Ladybug!

Ladybugs have very few enemies. Gardeners love them because they feast on aphids and other insects that attack plants. And the ladybugs' bright colors warn other insects to leave them alone. You see, ladybugs have a very nasty taste! Your students will enjoy creating and eating ladybug cookies as they further investigate these friends of the garden. However, unlike the real thing, these ladybugs are very tasty!

Ladybug Cookies

Ingredients:
1 vanilla wafer
mini chocolate chips
red-, yellow-, or orange-tinted frosting
thin black licorice

Directions:
Spread a layer of frosting on the wafer. Use a length of licorice to visually divide the cookie in half. Position mini chocolate-chip spots and licorice antennae. Yum!

Sarah Ann Lamb—Gr. 3, Lewis Carroll Elementary
Merritt Island, FL

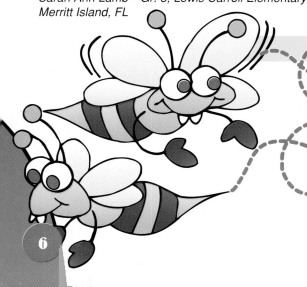

Busy Bees

Bring new meaning to the phrase "busy as bees" with a study of these ever busy insects. Bees—specifically honeybees—are the only insects that produce food eaten by man. Make a list of the different jobs that bees do; then have students compare the chores of these honey-makers to their daily jobs. Wow! Bees really are busy! The next time you have the opportunity to commend your youngsters for being as busy as bees, they'll know exactly what you mean!

Buggy Love

Writing poems about insects is twice as much fun when you collaborate with a partner! Set the mood by reading aloud a few of your favorite bug-related poems. If you're looking for a kid-pleasing collection of bug poems that blend factual information, a creative use of language, and a sharp sense of humor, you'll be delighted with *What To Do When A Bug Climbs In Your Mouth And Other Poems To Drive You Buggy,* written by Rick Walton and illustrated by Nancy Carlson (Lothrop, Lee & Shepard Books; 1995). At the conclusion of your oral poetry presentation, pair the youngsters and have each twosome pen a bug-related poem. Encourage students to write a variety of poetry. Or, if desired, display a format like the one shown for the students to follow. When the poems are written and illustrated, set aside time for each twosome to share its prose. Then bind the poems into a class book titled "We Love Bugs!"

We LOVE bugs!

_____ bugs,

_____ bugs,

Even _____ and _____ bugs.

We love *how* they_____.

We love *when* they_____.

We love *that* they_____.

We LOVE bugs!

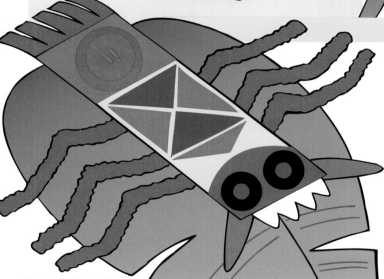

Inventing Insects

From *walking sticks* to *ladybugs,* insects have names, defenses, and disguises that are sure to fascinate your junior entomologists. After your young scientists have studied a variety of insects, they'll be ready to invent some never-before-heard-of bugs of their own! Provide a large selection of arts-and-crafts supplies that includes clothespins, buttons, felt, tissue paper, and pipe cleaners. Instruct each child to make a model of a newly discovered insect. Then give each child a large index card on which to write the name of her newfound bug and a description of its habitat and special features. Designate an area for youngsters to display their completed projects. By golly, your youngsters have created a bug museum!

Seven-Insect Story

If you're searching for a chapter book to share with your youngsters during your insect unit, *James And The Giant Peach* by Roald Dahl is a perfect choice. Even though James's insect traveling companions (seven in all) are fanciful in size, these delightful creatures reveal a bounty of facts about their true-to-life counterparts. As you read the story aloud, have each child record the bug-related facts he learns in a peach-shaped journal. By the conclusion of the story he'll have a peachy collection of bug facts!

Going BUGGY Over Books!

If your budding entomologists are bugging you for more information about bugs, check out these titles. In addition to a bounty of bug-related facts and trivia, this collection of books is teeming with impressive buggy close-ups!

The Icky Bug Counting Book

Written by Jerry Pallotta
Illustrated by Ralph Masiello
Charlesbridge Publishing, 1992

The colorful presentation of more than 25 different insects is enhanced with fun facts that heighten interest in bugs. Sharp details appear in well contrasted, accurate pictures. This appealing approach creates a wonderful reference for drawing and classifying bugs.

Monster Bugs

Written by Lucille Recht Penner
Illustrated by Pamela Johnson
Random House, Inc.; 1996

This Step Into Reading™ book is packed with amazing data about some of the world's largest and fiercest insects. Lifelike drawings invite close inspection of the critters, even though many of them are downright scary! Your bug enthusiasts are sure to latch onto this volume.

The Fascinating World Of...Beetles

Written by Maria Ángels Julivert
Illustrated by Marcel Socías Studios
Barron's Educational Series, Inc.; 1995

Even though only a portion of the 300,000 known species of beetles crawls across the pages of this buggy book, your students are sure to get an eyeful! Who would guess that beetles came in so many shapes, sizes, and colors? The world of the beetle is definitely fascinating and worth looking into during your study of insects.

Ants

Written by Ruth Berman
Photographed by William Muñoz
Lerner Publications Company, 1996

Hide the picnic basket! Here comes an army of the most awesome ant pictures ever collected. A cutaway view of an anthill, close-up shots of colonies, and information-packed text are featured in this Early Bird Nature Book. New science vocabulary is introduced in context.

Discover Hidden Worlds: Bugs

Written by Heather Amery and Jane Songi
Includes photographs
Western Publishing Company, Inc.; 1994

When is the last time you examined the sole of a housefly's foot, the eyes of a tsetse fly, or the jaws of a black garden ant? That's just a hint of what can be seen when you view the world of bugs through the lens of a microscope. Lively, fact-filled text and eye-opening photographs—some magnified thousands of times their actual size—take readers to a hidden world that cannot be seen by the naked eye. Your budding entomologists will be poring over the pages of this fascinating book again and again.

More Books About Bugs

Bugs And Other Insects
Written by Bobbie Kalman and Tammy Everts
Includes photographs
Crabtree Publishing Company, 1994

Butterflies, Bugs, And Worms
Written by Sally Morgan
Includes illustrations and photographs
Kingfisher, 1996

Creepy, Crawly Baby Bugs
Written by Sandra Markle
Includes photographs
Walker Publishing Company, Inc.; 1996

books reviewed by Deborah Zink Roffino

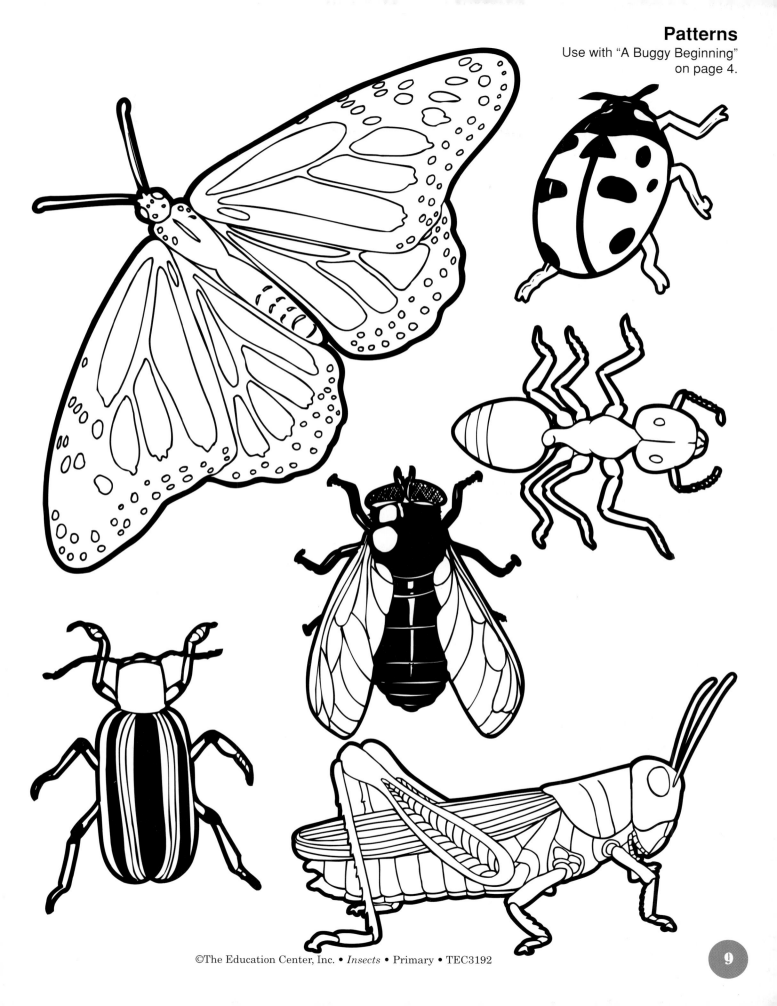

Name _____

Bug Watch

Carefully observe your bug. Follow the directions.

1. Write a number in each blank to tell how many parts your bug has:

___ head

___ abdomen

___ antennae

___ nose

___ mouth

___ thorax

___ legs

___ eyes

___ wings

___ skeleton

2. Illustrate your bug.

3. Watch your bug carefully. Write what it is doing.

4. Draw a picture of your bug's natural habitat.

©The Education Center, Inc. • *Insects* • Primary • TEC3192

Note To Teacher: Use this activity with "Checking Out Bugs" on page 5.

10

The Wonderful World Of Butterflies And Moths

With a zig and a zag, and a ziggety zag, flutter into the wonderful world of Lepidoptera! Explore the unusual life cycles, eating habits, and survival techniques of butterflies and moths with this high-flying unit.

ideas by Lucia Kemp Henry

Very Unique Insects

Did you know that no two butterflies or moths are exactly alike? It's a fact! And even more amazing is that there are approximately 165,000 different species of Lepidoptera. Like all insects, each butterfly or moth has three main body parts (head, thorax, abdomen), three pairs of jointed legs, and one pair of antennae. But it's their delicate wings that make them unique. Thousands of tiny scales cover the wing surfaces, creating the beautiful colors and patterns we often admire.

Introduce students to the wonderful world of Lepidoptera. For each student prepare an observation booklet by stapling together several blank sheets of 5" x 7" paper. Have students observe butterflies and moths, then draw and color their observations in their booklets. Plan nature walks or set aside small amounts of time to "watch." Encourage students to observe at home as well, then share their observations and illustrations with the class.

It Seems Like Magic!

All butterflies and moths pass through four stages of metamorphosis before they are fully grown. They begin their lives as eggs which hatch into hungry caterpillars. When each caterpillar reaches its full size, it surrounds itself with a protective case. After a period of time, the case splits open and an adult butterfly or moth emerges. The remarkable color photography in *Butterfly And Caterpillar* by Barrie Watts (Silver Burdett Company, 1985) clearly shows the complete life cycle and metamorphic stages of a butterfly.

Have students write about or illustrate the life cycles of several animals. As a class, categorize these animals: animals that have distinct changes in growth and those that do not. Students should conclude that animals experiencing metamorphosis or distinct changes (such as frogs, houseflies, and grasshoppers) are less common.

A World Without Lepidoptera?

If an environment is unhealthful, the butterflies and moths are affected. In fact, scientists often study butterflies and moths to determine the state of an environment. The habitats of Lepidoptera must be preserved in order to sustain the present number of butterflies and moths.

Plan a "Save the Lepidoptera" campaign. Have students make posters and buttons encouraging others to observe, rather than collect, butterflies and moths, and to discourage pollution and habitat destruction. Plan time for students to share existing or original poetry about these beautiful creatures. As a finale, invite a local nursery to help your class plant a Lepidoptera garden of wild or nectar-producing flowers. Encourage students to plant backyard Lepidoptera gardens as well.

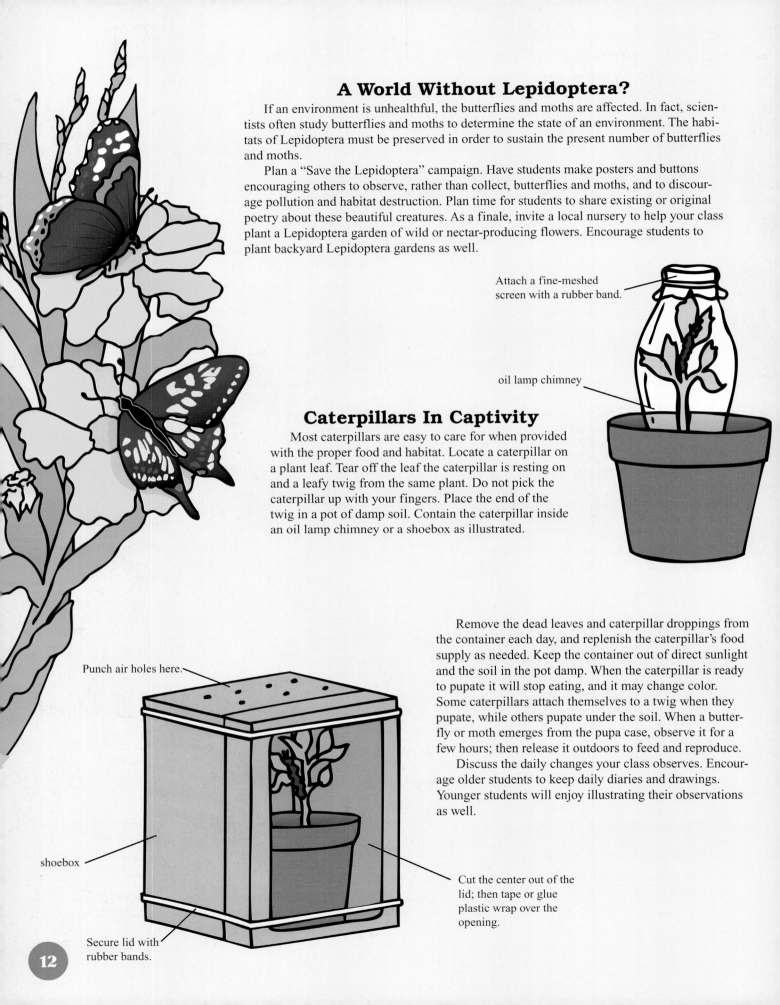

Attach a fine-meshed screen with a rubber band.

oil lamp chimney

Caterpillars In Captivity

Most caterpillars are easy to care for when provided with the proper food and habitat. Locate a caterpillar on a plant leaf. Tear off the leaf the caterpillar is resting on and a leafy twig from the same plant. Do not pick the caterpillar up with your fingers. Place the end of the twig in a pot of damp soil. Contain the caterpillar inside an oil lamp chimney or a shoebox as illustrated.

Remove the dead leaves and caterpillar droppings from the container each day, and replenish the caterpillar's food supply as needed. Keep the container out of direct sunlight and the soil in the pot damp. When the caterpillar is ready to pupate it will stop eating, and it may change color. Some caterpillars attach themselves to a twig when they pupate, while others pupate under the soil. When a butterfly or moth emerges from the pupa case, observe it for a few hours; then release it outdoors to feed and reproduce.

Discuss the daily changes your class observes. Encourage older students to keep daily diaries and drawings. Younger students will enjoy illustrating their observations as well.

Punch air holes here.

shoebox

Secure lid with rubber bands.

Cut the center out of the lid; then tape or glue plastic wrap over the opening.

12

Hungry Caterpillars

Caterpillars eat and eat and eat! Though some caterpillars are not choosy and eat a variety of plant foods, other caterpillars eat only one specific type of plant food. Have students discuss the advantages and disadvantages of a caterpillar eating only one type of plant food versus a variety of plant foods. *(Extinction would be more likely.)*

Post a chart containing the following information. Have students explain how this information could help them determine which butterflies and moths could be present in their backyards, in your local area, in urban areas, and in agricultural areas. Have students press and attach leaf samples to art paper before adding appropriate Lepidoptera illustrations.

Butterfly Caterpillar	Food
Buckeye	plantain
Cabbage White	mustard, cabbage family
Monarch	milkweed
Painted Lady	thistle
Common Sulphur	clover
Tiger Swallowtail	wild cherry

Moth Caterpillar	Food
Twin-spotted Sphinx	wild cherry, birch, willow
Achemon Sphinx	grape, Virginia creeper
Gypsy	shade trees
Luna	walnut, persimmon
Polyphemus	various trees
Acrea	leafy plants

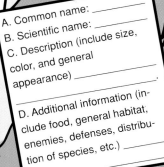

Lively Lepidoptera

Display these lively Lepidoptera projects zigging and zagging down a hallway. To make a moth, draw and color a large moth shape on a brown grocery bag or brown craft paper. Carefully crumple; then uncrumple the completed drawing. Repeat this procedure several times, until the paper is soft and wrinkled. Place the moth drawing between two sheets of clean paper and press with a warm iron. Allow the drawing to cool; then cut out the moth shape.

To create a crayon-resist butterfly, draw a large butterfly on art paper. Pressing firmly, color the butterfly shape with crayons. Dilute black tempera paint with water. Carefully paint over the completed butterfly drawing using long brush strokes. When the paint has dried, cut around the butterfly, leaving a small border.

Project Flutter!

Challenge students of all ages to create butterfly or moth projects to share with their class. Choose a report form appropriate for your students. Ask each student to create a display or an illustration to accompany his written report.

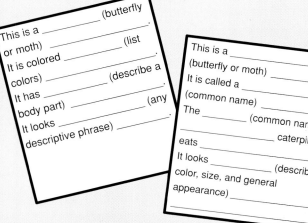

This is a _____ (butterfly or moth) _____
It is colored _____ (list colors) _____
It has _____ (describe a body part) _____
It looks _____ (any descriptive phrase) _____.

This is a _____ (butterfly or moth) _____
It is called a _____ (common name) _____
The _____ (common name) _____ caterpillar eats _____.
It looks _____ color, size, and general appearance) _____ (describe

A. Common name: _____
B. Scientific name: _____
C. Description (include size, color, and general appearance) _____
D. Additional information (include food, general habitat, enemies, defenses, distribution of species, etc.) _____

Display suggestions:

— an illustration using unusual media (sequins, tissue paper, fabric, yarn)
— a shoebox habitat
— a map showing the distribution of the species or its migration route
— a papier-mâché butterfly or moth
— a collection of original or published poetry about butterflies and moths

Name _____

Lots Of Changes

Butterflies and moths change a lot. They grow in stages. They look different at each stage. They begin life as **eggs.** Each egg hatches into a **caterpillar.** A caterpillar turns into a **pupa.** Then one day a **moth** or a **butterfly** comes out.

Here's how a **polyphemus moth** grows.
Write the name of each stage below the picture.
Use the **bold** words from the story.

_____   _____   _____   _____

How does a **monarch butterfly** grow and change?
Cut out the pictures and the words.
Glue them in order.

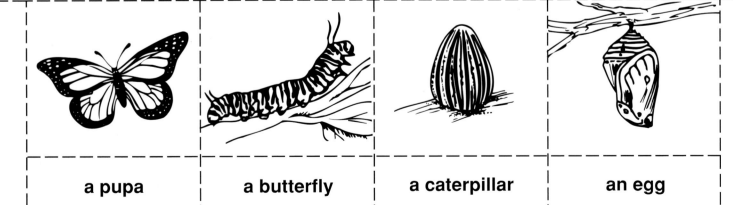

| a pupa | a butterfly | a caterpillar | an egg |

Bonus Box: Draw a puppy on the back of this sheet. Then draw the puppy as a grown dog. Look at your pictures. Does a puppy go through different stages like a butterfly or a moth?

Name _____

Which Is Which?

Butterflies and moths look alike. Sometimes it is hard to tell them apart. Most butterfly bodies are thin and smooth. And most moth bodies are fat and furry. But the best way to tell butterflies and moths apart is to look at their **antennae.** Moth antennae are feathery. Butterfly antennae have club-shaped ends.

Look at the pictures of the moth and the butterfly.
Read the words below the pictures.
If the words describe the moth picture, write **M** on the line.
If the words describe the butterfly picture, write **B** on the line.

Polyphemus Moth   **Monarch Butterfly**

_____ clubbed antennae   _____ fat body

_____ furry body   _____ feathery antennae

_____ many small dots   _____ smooth body

_____ thin body   _____ a few large spots

Sometimes you can tell a moth from a butterfly by its color. Most butterflies are more brightly colored. And most moths have duller colors. On the back of this sheet, draw and color a new kind of moth or butterfly. Try to use all the information you have learned. Give your moth or butterfly a name.

Bonus Box: Look in a book about butterflies and moths. Color the pictures of the polyphemus moth and the monarch butterfly.

An Extraordinary Butterfly

From metamorphosis to migration, the monarch butterfly is in a class all its own. Use the following activities to supplement your study of this fascinating flier.

ideas contributed by Ann Flagg

Getting Started: Making A Butterfly Nursery

Monarch butterflies can be raised and set free in most of the United States and southern Canada. A ten-gallon glass or plastic aquarium with a screen top makes a great butterfly nursery and observation center. If you live in an area where milkweed plants are plentiful, gather information on raising monarch butterflies (see the booklist on page 18); then carefully collect monarch caterpillars and a supply of milkweed for your nursery. Otherwise see page 18 for information on ordering monarch caterpillars and chrysalides.

Activity 1: Seeing Is Believing

You will need:
1 functioning butterfly nursery (see above)
several hand lenses

Each student will need:
1 construction-paper journal   pencil
   containing ten or more   crayons
   blank pages

What to do:
Have each student write "Monarch Moments" and his name on the front cover of his journal. Have small groups of students observe the butterfly nursery, using the hand lenses as needed. Then ask each child to date his first blank journal page and describe and/or illustrate what he saw. Set aside time for students to discuss their observations. Repeat the activity daily until each butterfly has hatched and been set free. Each day encourage students to discuss the changes they observe and make predictions about what will happen next.

Activity 2: An Amazing Metamorphosis

You will need:
1 functioning butterfly nursery (see "Getting Started" on this page)
1 butterfly life-cycle key like the one shown below
colorful markers
1 current calendar with large spaces for note taking

What to do:
Post the life-cycle key and the calendar in a student-accessible area. Encourage students to tell what they know about each stage of a butterfly's life. Next help the students determine what stage of life the nursery inhabitants are in. Ask one student to find the symbol for this stage on the life-cycle key. Ask another student to draw and color that symbol in the calendar space for that day. Each day before students go home (and the first thing Monday morning), have a volunteer update the calendar. After a butterfly emerges, have students determine the length of each stage that they observed. As an added challenge, have students use resource materials to determine the emerged butterfly's approximate date of birth.

This is why:

The life cycle of a monarch butterfly includes four stages: egg, caterpillar, pupa, *and* adult. *This four-stage process is called* metamorphosis. *Each egg is laid on a milkweed plant. In about three days, a caterpillar chews its way out of the egg and begins feeding on milkweed leaves. Each time the growing caterpillar becomes too big for its skin, it sheds the skin (or molts) and grows a new one. In about 9 to 14 days, the caterpillar is full size: about two inches long. The caterpillar spins a button of silk on the underside of a leaf and molts one last time. It emerges as a pupa. A hard shell called a* chrysalis *forms around the pupa. After about ten motionless days, this hard shell cracks open and an adult butterfly emerges. In about two hours, the flier's wings will be hardened, and it is ready to fly.*

Life-Cycle Key	
● =	egg
● =	caterpillar
● =	pupa
○ =	adult

Activity 3: Different Lives

Each student will need:

white construction-paper copy
   of the monarch cards on
   page 19

crayons and markers
scissors
envelope

What to do:

Have each student color and cut out his cards. Ask students to find four cards that show the metamorphosis of a monarch butterfly, arrange these cards chronologically (egg, caterpillar, pupa [chrysalis], adult), and number them from 1 to 4. Next tell the class that a butterfly drinks lots of nectar to gain strength; then it mates. Have students number the cards that show these steps "5" and "6" respectively. Then ask students to look for the card that shows an adult butterfly with an egg. Explain that when the adult female lays her eggs, the life cycle begins again. As students number this card "7," inform them that the lives of the adult butterflies are now over.

Next tell students that some monarchs live longer than others. Revisit cards 1 through 5 with your students. Explain that monarchs born late in summer do not mate right away. Instead they migrate or travel south for the winter (Card 5A). There they roost in trees (Card 5B) and wait for warmer temperatures and longer days. Eventually the monarchs begin their long trip home (Card 5C). The monarchs mate (Card 6), and the females lay their eggs (Card 7). Allow time for each student to practice telling the life story of a migrating monarch. Then have each child personalize his envelope and store his cards inside. Encourage students to use their cards to describe for their families what they've learned about the different lives of monarch butterflies.

This is why:

Like all butterflies, monarchs go through the four stages of development called metamorphosis. *In a summer this life cycle is repeated three or four times. The generation of summer monarchs born in the last cycle do not immediately mate. Instead they gather in large groups and fly south for the winter. In the spring the monarchs fly north toward their previous home and mate. Along the way the males die, the females lay their eggs and die, and the new eggs hatch. This new generation of butterflies continues the northward journey. A monarch that migrates lives about eight or nine months. A monarch that does not migrate lives only about three to five weeks.*

Activity 4: Migrating Monarchs

Each student will need:

copy of monarch markers on page 19
copy of page 20
crayons or markers
scissors
glue

What to do:

Remind students why milkweed is important to the monarch butterfly. Have each student study his map and map key. Lead students to conclude that monarchs can live throughout the continental United States and in southern Canada, where milkweed is plentiful. (Monarchs also live in other parts of the world.) Have each student randomly color orange dots on his map to show monarch homes in the continental United States, then color his map key to match. Next tell students that monarchs migrate to winter roosting sites along the California coast and in the mountains of Mexico. Have each student randomly color black dots on his map to show roosting sites in each of these locations, then color his map key to match.

Next ask each student to find the Rocky Mountains on his map. Explain that monarchs living west of the Rocky Mountains migrate to California and that monarchs living east of the Rocky Mountains migrate to Mexico. Ask each student to use a green crayon to show possible migration routes on his map, then color the map key to match.

Lastly have each student color and cut out his seven monarch markers. Instruct students to read each sentence in the border. If a sentence is true, a student does nothing. If a sentence is not true, he glues a monarch marker on top of it. *(Answer key: In both the right and left borders, facts and illustrations alternate.)*

This is why:

Monarch butterflies cannot survive cold temperatures. So when summer temperatures begin to cool and the days begin to shorten, the last monarchs of the summer season instinctively know to migrate south. Large groups of monarchs may travel up to 2,000 miles to their winter roosts. Scientists are amazed how these migrating butterflies, that have never before flown south, can find their way to the same winter homes that previous generations of monarchs have occupied.

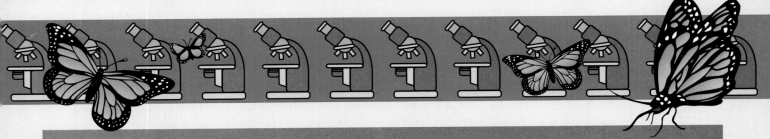

More About Monarchs

Use the following resources to enhance your study of monarch butterflies.

Ordering Information

Let's Get Growing
1-800-408-1868
Monarch caterpillars with milkweed plants are available for purchase. Catalog and ordering information available upon request.

Insect Lore
1-800-LIVE-BUG
Monarch caterpillars are available for purchase in kits of varying sizes.

Monarch Watch
1-888-TAGGING
Two types of Monarch-rearing kits are available for purchase by schools and individuals living east of the Rocky Mountains. Call toll-free for more information.

Internet Sites

Monica The Monarch
http://www2.cybernex.net/~dbenz/monarch.htm
This site, created by a sixth-grade student and her father, has beautiful photographs and easy-to-understand text that describe the life cycle of a Monarch butterfly named Monica.

Monarch Watch
http://www.monarchwatch.org/
You'll find a wealth of information about the Monarch butterfly. Topics include Monarch Biology, Rearing Monarchs, Milkweed, Monarchs In The Classroom, and Tagging Monarchs.

Books About Monarchs

Monarch Butterfly
Written & Illustrated by Gail Gibbons
Holiday House, Inc.; 1991

An Extraordinary Life: The Story Of A Monarch Butterfly
Written by Laurence Pringle & Illustrated by Bob Marstall
Orchard Books, 1997

Monarch Butterflies
Written by Emilie U. Lepthien & Includes photographs
Childrens Press®, Inc.; 1989

Monarch Cards And Markers

Use the monarch cards with "Activity 3: Different Lives" on page 17.

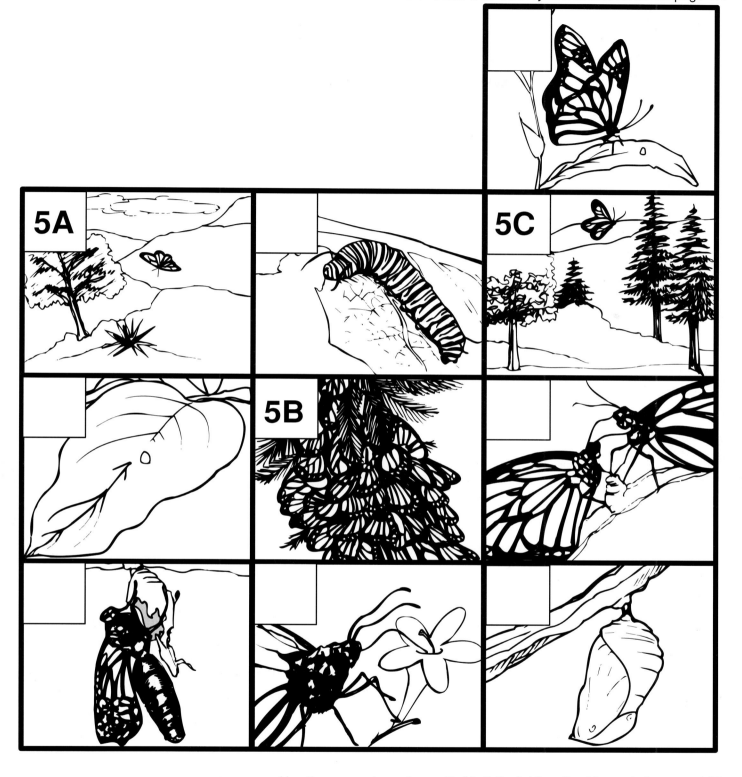

Use the monarch markers with "Activity 4: Migrating Monarchs" on page 17.

Migrating Monarchs

Monarchs have six legs.

Monarchs only live in Texas.

A monarch weighs less than a penny!

Monarchs sip nectar.

A monarch lays its eggs in trees.

Monarchs go south in fall.

Monarchs go north in spring.

A monarch lives about one year.

Some monarchs live longer than others.

Monarchs like cold weather.

A caterpillar hatches from a monarch egg.

Monarchs need trees.

Monarch caterpillars eat milkweed.

A butterfly hatches from a monarch egg.

A female monarch lays about 400 eggs.

Monarchs do not fly at night.

In winter monarchs gather in large groups.

Only monarchs migrate.

Monarchs can migrate 2,000 miles!

All monarchs migrate to Mexico.

Monarchs are orange and black.

CANADA

Northern Limit Of Milkweed

Rocky Mountains

California

UNITED STATES

MEXICO

Map Key
◯ = monarch home
◯ = winter roosting sites
╱ = possible migration routes
∧∧∧ = mountains

Name _____

BUG BONANZA

Strike it rich with these ideas to turn an ordinary day into a fun-filled bug bonanza!

ideas by Mary Dinneen and Lori Bruce

slender grasshopper
quickly hops
long legs
moving jaw
delicate wings
suddenly flies

"Pardner Poems"

Some "buggy" observations will lead students to create these delightful word pair poems. First have students observe some bugs and name some of their characteristics. On the chalkboard, create a word bank of these characteristics. Next introduce the format shown and have each student create a "pardner poem." Encourage students to refer to the word bank for additional inspiration.

Line 1:   one word that describes and one word that names your bug

Line 2–6:   one word that describes and one word that names a characteristic of your bug

Buggy Buddies

Your buckaroos can keep these bug creations corralled indefinitely! Challenge students to design bugs that resemble the bugs they observed. To make a bug, select a section of egg carton, a fast-food container, or a piece of disposable dinnerware for the body. Add body features and a head using scraps of construction paper, wallpaper, waxed paper, poster board, or felt. For antennae, wrap the midsection of a pipe cleaner around a brad. Insert the brad through the top of the body; then secure the brad and shape the pipe cleaner as desired. Attach six poster-board legs. Crease each leg to form joints. Weight the legs by taping a penny or similar object near the bottom of each. Embellish the critter with glitter and ribbon, if desired.

To make a "bug leash," knot a two-foot length of elastic thread. Using a blunt needle, poke the thread length up through the underside of the bug body. Showcase your students' creative talents during a bug parade. Onlooking eyes are certain to "bug out" as your students and their bouncing bugs make their debut!

Getting The Bugs Out

Students will enjoy getting the bugs out of "buggy" math problems! Write a variety of math problems with their corresponding answers on the chalkboard. In each problem, cover one numeral (each time it occurs) with a colorful bug cutout. Have students copy the problems and answers on their papers, replacing the "bugs" with the missing numerals. When appropriate, remove the cutouts from the displayed problems and have students check their work.

Fluttery Snacks

Your youngsters are sure to go buggy over these yummy butterfly bites!

Ingredients:
1 celery stick per student
twist pretzels (2 per student)
spreadable cheddar cheese

creamy peanut butter
raisins
broken pretzel pieces

Directions:
Fill a celery stick with cheese or peanut butter. Press two twist-pretzel wings in place. Add two pretzel-piece antennae and two raisin eyes. Enjoy!

Jan Coxon—Gr. 1, Harrisburg Academy, Wormleysburg, PA

Flamboyant Flutterer

Begin a butterfly project by wrapping a toilet-tissue or paper-towel tube with construction paper that has been cut to fit the tube. Using glue, markers, and scraps of construction paper, add facial features and antennae to the tube to complete the butterfly's body. For the wings, trace a wing-half pattern onto folded tagboard as shown. Cut along the resulting outline, leaving the fold intact. Unfold the tagboard. If a specific pattern is desired on the wings, draw a matching design on each side of the fold. Cover the design with tissue-paper squares by repeating the following method: Center the eraser end of a pencil over a small tissue-paper square. Wrap the paper upward around the pencil. Holding the paper in place, dip it in glue and press it onto the desired location. When the design is completely covered with tissue paper and the glue has dried, staple the butterfly body to the wings. Suspend this butterfly from the ceiling so that it can really flutter around.

Rita Arnold, Alden Hebron, Woodstock, IL

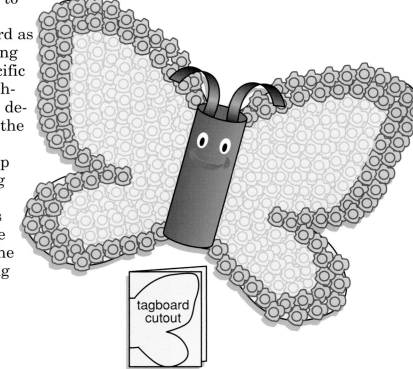

tagboard
cutout

Crawly Ideas

All Aflutter!

These eye-catching butterflies can be created in just a flit and a flutter! Invert a small-size disposable soup bowl; then use colorful tempera paints to paint the bottom of the bowl. While the paint is drying, trim four 4 1/2" x 6" sheets of construction paper to resemble butterfly wings and two 2" x 4" strips of black construction paper to resemble butterfly antennae. Arrange the wing and antennae cutouts so that they achieve the desired results when the inverted bowl is in place. Glue together all overlapping surfaces of the wing and antennae cutouts, creating one large shape. Squeeze a trail of glue around the rim of the bowl; then invert the bowl on the construction-paper shape. Gently press on the bowl until the glue dries. Now that's a colorful flier!

Doris Hautala—Gr. 3, Washington Elementary, Ely, MN

Folded Flyers

Your recycling enthusiasts are going to love making these eye-catching butterflies! To make a butterfly, tear two brightly colored pages from a discarded magazine. Fold one page in half; then trace the half-pattern on page 28 onto the page. Cut on the resulting outline—not on the fold. Next unfold the paper and refold it so that the rounded ends meet. Starting at the fold and working toward one rounded end, accordion fold one-half of the pattern. Fold the remaining half of the pattern in the same manner; then set the piece aside. Next cut a 6 1/2-inch square from the second magazine page. Fold the square in half, making a triangle. Starting at the fold and working outward, accordion fold one-half of the pattern. Fold the remaining half of the pattern in the same manner. Join the two folded pattern pieces with a length of black pipe cleaner as shown; then gently spread the wings of the butterfly. There you have it! A one-of-a-kind folded flyer!

Donna Dayer—Gr. 2
Anne Watson Elementary
Conway, AR

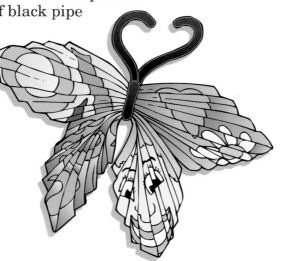

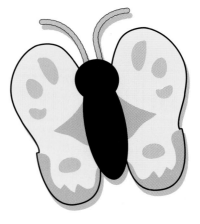

Bat Your Wings!

No doubt your students will jump into this butterfly project with both feet! To make a butterfly, have each student trace the outlines of both of his shoes onto construction paper and cut them out. Transform the foot cutouts into wings by gluing them to a black construction-paper butterfly body (pattern on page 29) as shown. Glue on pipe cleaner antennae. Display these flutterers around the classroom.

Sharon Haley, Jacksonville, NC

Ladybug Wind Sock

Ladybug, Ladybug! Please dance and twirl in the wind! This adorable project, made from a pair of ladybug designs, is sure to delight your students.

For each wind sock you need:
— construction paper as follows:
  - two 10" red circles (body)
  - two 10" black circles (body)
  - two 4 1/2" x 6" strips of black (dots)
  - two 6" black circles (head)
  - four 3" x 4" strips of black (antennae)
  - four 2" black circles (eyes)
  - four 3" yellow circles (eyes)
  - one 9" x 12" sheet of black

— six 2-foot black crepe-paper streamers
— 4-foot length of yarn for hanging
— hole puncher
— scissors
— glue

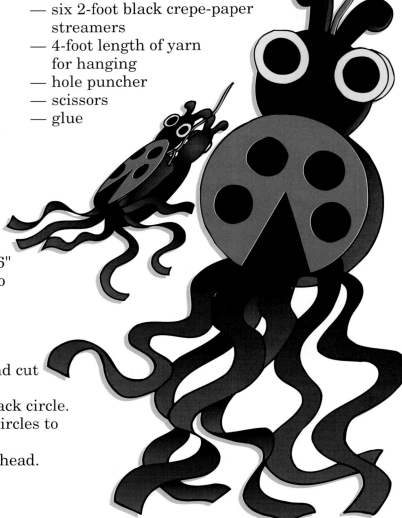

To make two bodies:
1. Cut a pie wedge from one red circle.
2. Glue the red circle atop a ten-inch black circle.
3. Cut several small circles from a 4 1/2" x 6" strip of black paper. Glue these cutouts to the red circle.
4. Repeat steps one through three.

To make two heads:
1. Stack two 3" x 4" strips of black paper and cut out two antenna shapes.
2. Glue the antenna shapes to a six-inch black circle.
3. For eyes, glue two of the two-inch black circles to two yellow circles.
4. Glue the resulting eyes on the ladybug's head.
5. Repeat steps one through four.

To complete the project:
1. Glue each completed head to a completed body.
2. Glue the six crepe-paper streamers to a long edge of the 9" x 12" sheet of black paper; then roll the paper into a cylinder. Glue.
3. Glue the cylinder between the two ladybug projects. (See the illustration.)
4. Punch two holes near the top and on opposite sides of the cylinder. Thread one yarn end through the holes and knot it so that one end of the yarn can be used to suspend the project.
5. Center the yarn between the antennae and glue the top part of each pair of eyes together.

Doris M. Hautala—Gr. 3, Washington Elementary School, Ely, MN

Shimmery Dragonflies

A display of these dazzling dragonflies is sure to attract plenty of attention! To make a dragonfly, fold a 9" x 12" sheet of white construction paper in half (to 4 1/2" x 12"). Place a tagboard template of the pattern on page 29 on the folded paper as shown; then trace around the shape and cut along the resulting outline. Unfold the cutout. Working atop a newspaper-covered surface, use tempera paint to paint the cutout as desired. Sprinkle the wet paint with glitter. Or wait for the paint to dry, brush a thin layer of diluted glue over the project, and sprinkle glitter atop the glue. Mount the dazzling dragonfly on a 9" x 12" sheet of construction paper before putting it on display. Spectacular!

Allison Haynes, Lexington, NC

A Compound Collection

This butterfly collection provides practice naming, spelling, and dividing compound words. Use the pattern to prepare several construction-paper butterflies. Glue pictures of compound words on the butterfly bodies. Program the backs to show how the words are spelled and divided. Laminate the butterfly cutouts for durability. Fold and paper clip the wings of each butterfly before placing them in a decorated container.

The student retrieves a butterfly from the container and names the compound word shown. He then writes the word on his paper and draws a line to separate the two words of the compound. To check his work, he unclips the butterfly wings.

Mary Howard, San Antonio, TX

Pattern

Compound Word List

eyebrow	flashlight	thumbtack
lipstick	starfish	sidewalk
cowboy	scarecrow	baseball
rainbow	doorknob	popcorn
cupcake	airplane	notebook
suitcase	toothbrush	fireplace
shoelace	handcuff	peanut

Butterfly Booklets

Watch your students' writing skills take flight with these appealing butterfly booklets. To begin, have students research and compile information about butterflies. Then ask each student to use his new knowledge to write a butterfly-related story or poem. As you guide students through the writing process, compare the process to the metamorphosis of a butterfly. Explain that, just as a butterfly must go through several stages before it is ready to take flight, writing must go through several stages before it is ready to be published. As each student reaches the final-draft stage, have him copy his writing onto wing-shaped papers and bind the resulting pages between two similarly shaped poster-board covers. (Provide assistance as needed.) To embellish his booklet, have the student attach pipe-cleaner antennae and decorate his booklet cover to resemble an actual butterfly. Encourage students to share their writing projects with each other. Then suspend the butterfly booklets from the ceiling and watch them flutter into flight.

Arlene Stoebner, Lincoln School, Yankton, SD

25

Ladybug Time

After reading *The Grouchy Ladybug* by Eric Carle, use red poster board and black construction paper to create a giant-size booklet cover like the one shown. Using a stamp pad and a clock stamp, print a clock face on each of several booklet pages. Program one page for each hour of the school day. Then, on each page, write a class-generated description of the activities that normally take place during that hour. Next give each page to a small group of students to be illustrated. Finally sequence the completed pages and staple them inside the booklet cover. Older students will enjoy making personalized mini-versions of this timely booklet.

Elizabeth A. Main—Gr. 1, Davenport Elementary School
Davenport, FL

Buggy Over Fractions

These adorable ladybugs make fraction practice a friendly experience. Enlarge the ladybug pattern on page 28 to a desired size; then duplicate ten copies of the pattern on red construction paper. Number the ladybug patterns from one to ten, and attach a different set of two colors of sticky dots to each ladybug. Laminate and cut out the patterns; then program the backs of the cutouts for self-checking. Store the ladybugs in a resealable plastic bag. Place the bag of cutouts, pencils, and a supply of paper at a center. A student numbers his paper from 1 to 10. For each ladybug, the student determines what fractional part of the dot set each color of dot represents. (For example, if there are two blue dots and four yellow dots, 2/6 of the set is blue and 4/6 of the set is yellow.) He writes his answers on his paper; then he flips the cutout to check his work. He continues in this manner until he has completed the center.

Mary Taylor—Gr. 2, Sun Prairie, WI

Barry

1. ⅓ is blue.
   ⅔ is yellow.
2. ³⁄₆ is green.
   ³⁄₆ is purple.

These busy bees are buzzing with accomplishments! Using the pattern on page 30, have students color and cut out bees. Tape pipe-cleaner antennae and yellow cellophane wings to the backs of the bees. (Add dimension to the wings by gathering the cellophane before taping.) Each student then writes one special accomplishment for the school year. Have students cut speech bubbles around their writing, then display the speech bubbles alongside their bees on the bulletin board.

Judy Peterson, Delta, UT

Keep students buzzing with good attendance all year long! Mount a hive cutout and the title as shown. Using construction-paper copies of the bee patterns on page 30, have each student decorate and cut out a bee. Store the cutouts. Each time 100 percent attendance (or another agreed-upon goal) is achieved, attach a bee cutout to the display. Periodically recognize your youngsters' efforts with a special class privilege.

Tonya Byrd—Gr. 2, William Owen Elementary, Fayetteville, NC

Patterns

Use ladybug pattern with
"Buggy Over Fractions"
on page 26.

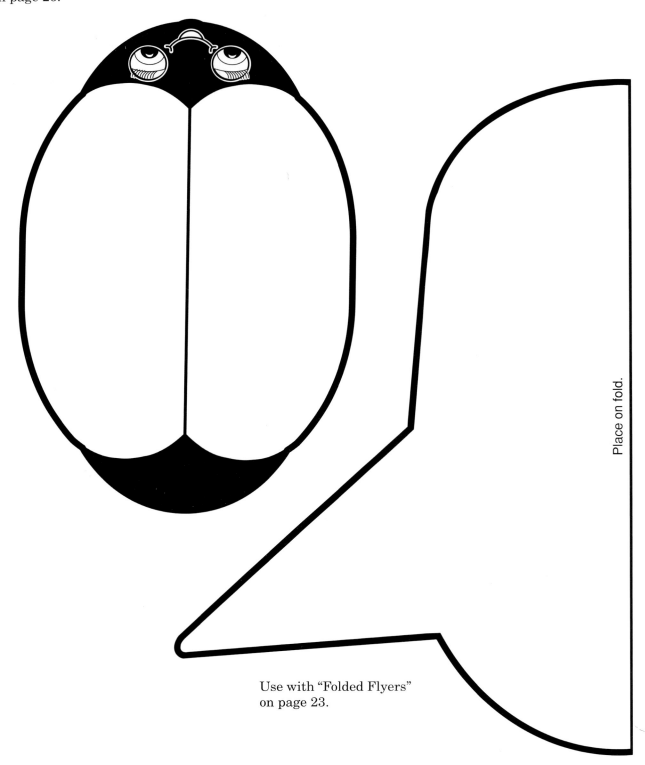

Place on fold.

Use with "Folded Flyers"
on page 23.

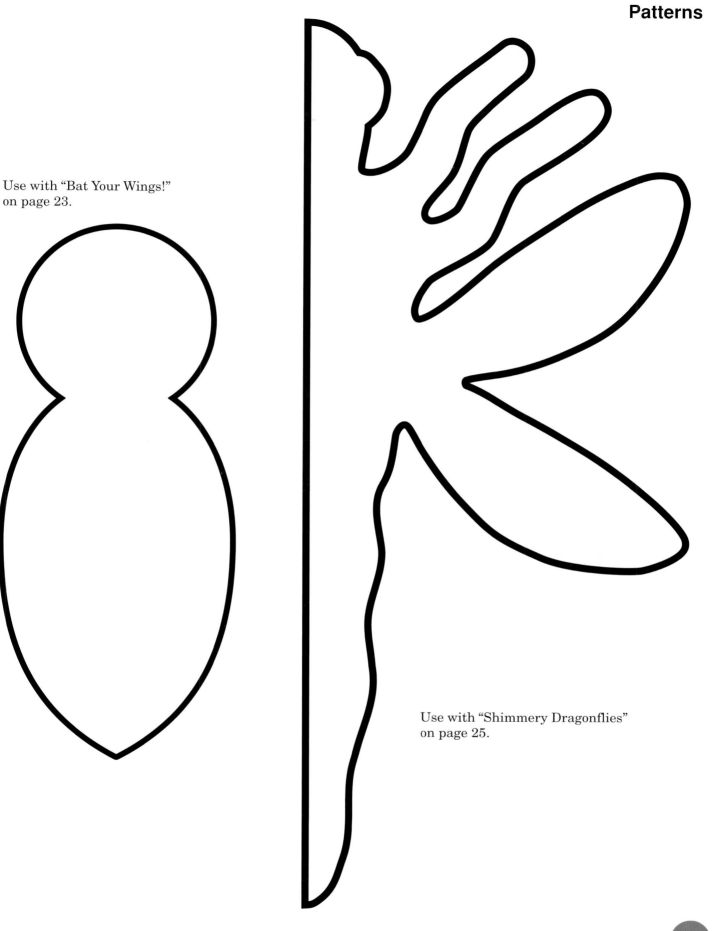

Use with "Bat Your Wings!"
on page 23.

Use with "Shimmery Dragonflies"
on page 25.

Patterns

Use bees with
"We're Buzzing…"
on page 27.

Use with "We've
Been Busy
Bees!"
on page 27.

Reproducible Activities...

from Teacher's Helper® magazine.

Investigating Insects Unit

Background For The Teacher
Insects

The definition of insects is simple enough: small, six-legged creatures with bodies divided into three main parts. This, however, is the only simple part of the world of insects.

There are over 800,000 types of insects known currently (compared to 200,000 kinds of other animals). Each year 7,000–10,000 new kinds of insects are discovered. This means that, for every one kind of animal, there are four kinds of insects. And the total number of insects in one square mile of land equals the entire human population of the world.

Then there's the staggering variety of insects. Though most are less than 1/4 inch, insects can be as small as 1/100 inch (fairy fly) and as large as 10 inches (Atlas moth's wingspread). Some look like leaves, sticks, and thorns.

Since insects are thought to have lived 400 million years ago, it's obvious that they are adept at surviving. But how is it that they've been able to thrive so well? Scientists reason that insects adapt quickly to the cruellest of environments (some start their lives in crude oil); the small size of an insect gives it advantages; most insects have wings, giving them greater maneuverability; and the skeleton of an insect is on the outside, providing better protection.

Answer Key For Page 33

Answer Key For Page 34

Name _____

Buggy Paragraphs

Read each paragraph.
Draw a line through the sentence that does not belong.

An insect is a small animal. Insect bodies are made **in sect**ions. All insects have three body sections. An elephant is gray and has a trunk. They have a head, a thorax and an abdomen.

All insects have eyes, antennae, and a mouth on their heads. Insects have three pairs of legs and sometimes they have wings on their thorax. Birds use wings to fly. An insect's abdomen has no legs or wings.

Insects do not have backbones. Instead they have a hard outside skeleton. There are many beautiful butterflies. When a young insect grows, it sheds its skeleton. Then the insect's soft, new skin becomes hard.

Many insects go through four life stages. First an insect lays eggs. Then the eggs hatch into larvae. The larvae look like worms. The larva turns into a pupa. Look closely to see the antennae. Finally, the adult insect may look like a butterfly or a housefly.

Some insects can sing. The insects sing by rubbing their legs or wings together. Many insect mouths have a tube. Singing or chirping helps these insects find a mate.

Some insects are pests. Mosquitoes "bite" people. They feed on human blood. First a mosquito stabs the skin. Then it thins the blood with saliva. It fills its stomach and flies away fast! At last the dinosaurs died.

Some insects are hard to see. They are the same color as their surroundings. Trees provide homes for many animals. Some insects look like other animals or things. These tricks help them stay alive.

Bees are insects. Worker bees look for nectar and pollen. They tell other bees where to find food by dancing. Ants are social insects. When the food is good, the worker bee dances long and hard!

Bonus Box: Make a list of five different insects on the back of this sheet. Then draw a picture of each insect on your list.

Name _____

Insect Fact And Fantasy

Read each sentence.
If it could happen, color the object.
If it could not happen, do not color the object.

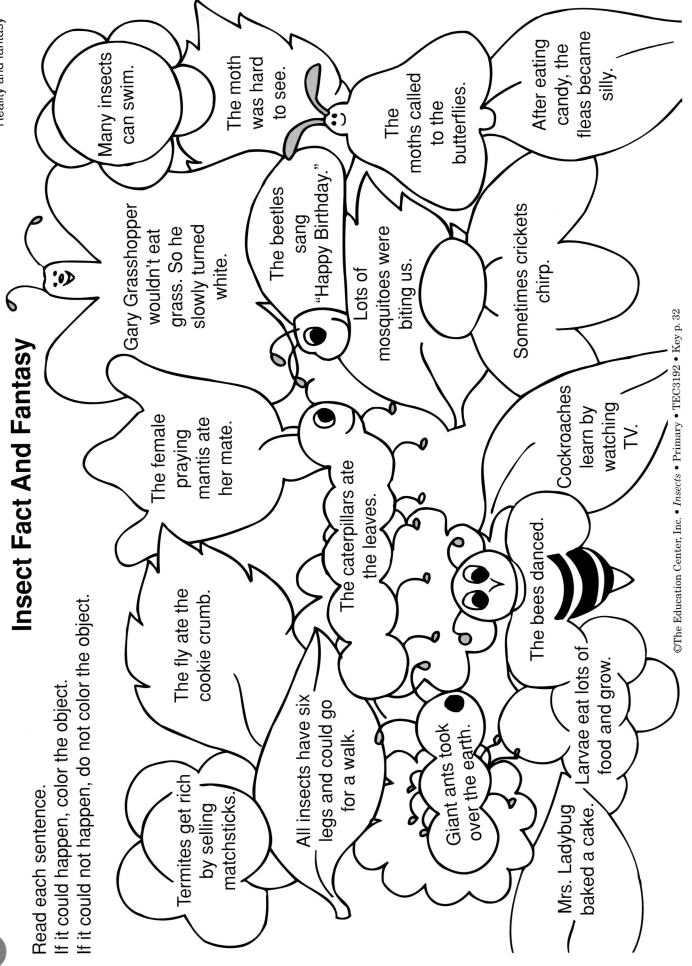

Many insects can swim.

The moth was hard to see.

The moths called to the butterflies.

After eating candy, the fleas became silly.

Gary Grasshopper wouldn't eat grass. So he slowly turned white.

The beetles sang "Happy Birthday."

Lots of mosquitoes were biting us.

Sometimes crickets chirp.

The female praying mantis ate her mate.

The caterpillars ate the leaves.

Cockroaches learn by watching TV.

The fly ate the cookie crumb.

The bees danced.

Termites get rich by selling matchsticks.

All insects have six legs and could go for a walk.

Giant ants took over the earth.

Larvae eat lots of food and grow.

Mrs. Ladybug baked a cake.

34

A Buggy Friend

Follow the directions.

1. Cut along the dotted lines.
2. Fold the paper in half on the light line.
3. Cut along the dark line.
4. Unfold the insect.
5. Draw and color two big eyes on the head.
6. Color the head any color you wish.
7. Draw and color polka dots on the thorax.
8. Draw and color stripes on the abdomen.

Bonus Box: Draw a picture of flowers on another sheet of paper. Glue your buggy friend on your picture.

Lovely Ladybugs Unit

How To Use Page 37

1. Read a ladybug-related book (see "Related Literature: Ladybugs" on this page).
2. Then distribute a copy of page 37 to each student.
3. Ask each child to write about one of the following topics:
   — why ladybugs are helpful to farmers and gardeners
   — the life cycle of a ladybug
   — how it would feel to be a ladybug
   — a meal with a ladybug family
   — what a ladybug sees while it is flying

Variations

— Program this sheet to review ladybug vocabulary.
— Use it as a spelling test paper.
— Have students complete the extension activity on this page and write an invented recipe for a new edible insect.

Related Literature
Ladybugs

Ladybug
Written by Emery Bernhard
Illustrated by Durga Bernhard
Published by Holiday House, Inc.

Ladybug, Ladybug
Written & Illustrated by Ruth Brown
Published by Dutton Children's Books

Ladybug On The Move
Written & Illustrated by Richard Fowler
Published by Harcourt Brace Jovanovich, Publishers

The Grouchy Ladybug
Written & Illustrated by Eric Carle
Published by Scholastic Inc.

The Ladybug And Other Insects
Created by Gallimard Jeunesse & Pascale de
   Bourgoing
Illustrated by Sylvie Perols
Published by Scholastic Inc.

What About Ladybugs?
Written & Illustrated by Celia Godkin
Published by Sierra Club Books For Children

Background For The Teacher
Ladybugs

The ladybug (otherwise known as a ladybug beetle) is a small beetle with a tiny round body. It typically has bright red or yellow outer wings with black, red, white, or yellow spots. Ladybugs are helpful to growers and gardeners because they eat aphids—plant-eating insects.

The development of ladybugs begins with bright yellow eggs laid by the female after she mates. After about one week, larvae hatch from the eggs. The larvae consume many aphids at this time. After the larvae *molt*—or shed their skin—five times, they enter the pupa stage. During this stage, they produce a protective covering and then change into adults. In approximately one week, the adult ladybug emerges from its shell. It will spend its short life eating and producing eggs to continue the life cycle.

Extension Activity
Ladybugs

Use this tasty recipe to treat your students to an edible ladybug. For each child you will need:
   1 paper plate
   1/2 apple
   1 lettuce leaf
   1 grape
   8–12 raisins
   1 tablespoon peanut butter

Have each child place his lettuce leaf on a paper plate; then have him place the apple half (cut side down) on the lettuce leaf. Next have each student use peanut butter to attach the grape—the ladybug's head—as shown. Finally have each child use peanut butter to attach two raisins to the grape for eyes; then have her use peanut butter to attach the remaining raisins on the apple as the ladybug's spots.

Name _____

Ladybug Tales

Lovely Ladybugs Unit

Materials Needed For Each Student:
— a copy of page 39
— crayons
— scissors
— 1 piece of 4 1/2" x 12" red construction paper
— 1 red construction-paper copy of the ladybug wings on this page
— 1 black, 6" pipe cleaner
— a 1 1/2" black pom-pom
— 2 wiggle eyes
— 1 brad
— glue
— black marker (optional)

Finished Sample

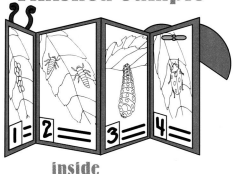

inside

front

back

How To Use Page 39 To Make A Ladybug Minibooklet

1. Introduce students to ladybugs by reading *The Ladybug And Other Insects* by Gallimard Jeunesse and Pascale de Bourgoing (Scholastic Inc.) or other selections from "Related Literature: Ladybugs" (page 36). Use the information in "Background For The Teacher: Ladybugs" on page 36 to teach your students about the *metamorphosis,* or transformation, of a ladybug.

2. Next read the sentences on page 39 with your students; then have each child number the boxes to sequence the stages of a ladybug's life.

3. Have each student color the picture in each box and cut along the heavy solid lines.

4. Next demonstrate for your students how to accordion-fold the red paper into four equal sections as shown. Have each child fold his paper into four sections as instructed.

5. Next ask each student to unfold the red paper and glue the four metamorphic stages in order on the sections.

6. With the booklet closed again, have each child use glue to attach his ladybug's antennae (bent pipe cleaner) to the cover of his minibooklet.

7. Then ask each student to glue his pom-pom atop the base of the antennae for the head as shown.

8. Finally have him glue the eyes to the pom-pom to complete the cover.

9. To finish the book, have each student cut the wings on the heavy solid lines. Then have him push a brad through the dot at the top of each wing and through the book's back cover near the top. Have the student use a marker to draw dots on the wings if desired.

Wing Patterns

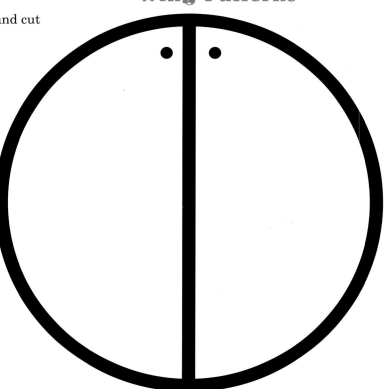

Changing Ladybugs

Number these pictures to show how a ladybug grows.
Color.
Cut.

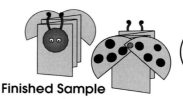

Finished Sample

Use this sheet to make a lady-bug minibooklet!

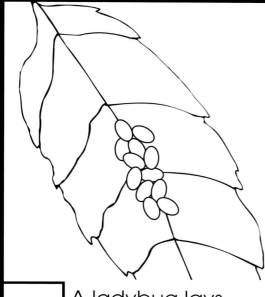

A ladybug lays many bright yellow eggs.

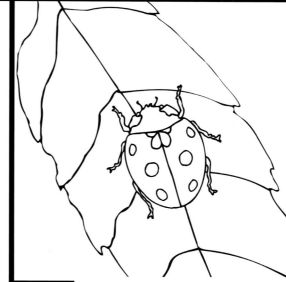

A ladybug hatches from each hard shell.

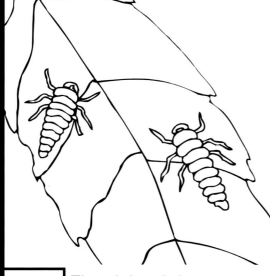

Tiny black larvae hatch from the eggs.

Each larva wraps up in a hard shell to become a pupa.

The Buzz About Bees Unit

How To Use Page 41 To Make A Bee Booklet

1. Introduce the topic of bees by inviting an apiarist to your classroom. Ask the apiarist to discuss the benefits of bees or how honey is made and collected. Or share with your students excerpts from a factual book such as *Life Of The Honeybee*.
2. Give each student a copy of page 41. Ask each student to cut the booklet on the heavy black lines. Have the student sequence the booklet cover and pages. Staple each student's booklet together along the left-hand side.
3. Guide students in reading about bees and some of their characteristics.

Related Literature

Bees

Life Of The Honeybee
Written by Heiderose and Andreas Fischer-Nagel
Published by Carolrhoda Books, Inc.

The Life Cycle Of The Honeybee
Written by Paula Z. Hogan
Illustrated by Geri K. Strigenz
Published by Raintree Publishers Inc.

From Blossom To Honey
Written by Ali Mitgutsch
Published by Carolrhoda Books, Inc.

Honeybee
Written by Barrie Watts
Published by Silver Burdett Press

Honeybee's Busy Day
Written by Richard Fowler
Published by Doubleday

Background For The Teacher

Bees

Honeybees live together in an organized group called a colony. Their home is called a hive. There are three types of bees in the colony—the queen bee, workers, and drones. Each type of bee has its own job to do. The queen bee is a fertile female who can lay eggs. Worker bees are females, but they do not lay eggs. Worker bees engage in tasks such as building the honeycomb, feeding the growing bees, cleaning the hive, collecting food and water, and defending the hive from other creatures. The drones are male and their sole purpose is to mate with the queen bee. Drones die shortly thereafter. They cannot help the workers take care of the hive, so they are stung to death, left to starve, or driven away. In this way the colony's precious food is not wasted on noncontributing members.

Honeybees are helpful in many ways. As bees gather pollen from flowers to take back to the hive and store as food, it is often transferred from one blossom to another blossom of the same type. This is how bees help pollinate blossoms. Only after pollination occurs can fertilization take place. Once fertilized, plants can produce fruit or seeds. Bees also are able to make honey from the nectar that they collect. Nectar is a sweet, sugary juice found in flowers. Worker bees suck this substance from flowers and store it in their crops—or honey stomachs. After the honeybees have collected as much nectar as they can carry, they return to the hive where the nectar is regurgitated. The nectar is spread in a cell or given to other worker bees. During this process enzymes are added to the nectar. It is also very warm in the hive, so water evaporates from the nectar. The addition of enzymes and the evaporation of water from the nectar turns it into honey.

Cut. Staple. Read.

The Buzz About Bees

Name _____

Honeybees live in
a hive.

⬡ 1

A hive has one
queen bee.

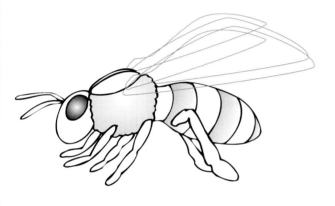

⬡ 2

Other bees that live in the hive
are called **workers** and **drones.**

⬡ 3

Worker bees get **nectar**
and **pollen** from flowers.

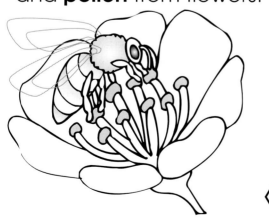

⬡ 4

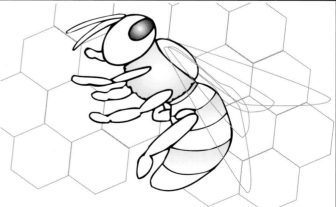

Bees make honey from
the nectar.

⬡ 5

Best Buzzer Award

Queenie Bee is about to announce the winner of the Best Buzzer Award. To find out which bee has won:

Read each sentence.
Find the bees that cannot be the winner.
Draw an X on each of them.
Circle the bee that has won.

1. The bee does not have straight antennae.
2. The bee has an odd number of dark stripes.
3. The bee has round eyes.
4. The bee does not have spots on its wings.
5. The bee is smiling.

Bonus Box: On the back of this sheet, draw a picture of the winning bee holding its award.

©The Education Center, Inc. • *Insects* • Primary • TEC3192

The
"Buzz" Word
Is…

_____

Had a
Gr-r-reat
Day!

©The Education Center, Inc. • *Insects* • Primary • TEC3192

Buzzzzz....

Look who is
buzzing along
with _____!

_____
child's name

_____
teacher

_____
date

©The Education Center, Inc. • *Insects* • Primary • TEC3192

All Aflutter With Poetry Unit

Materials Needed For Each Student:

crayons
scissors
glue

How To Use Page 45

Give each student a white construction-paper copy of page 45. Allow time for student pairs to complete the reproducible. Then, in small groups, have students share several word possibilities for each letter. Encourage students to fill in any blanks they may have. Have students complete their butterfly projects using the directions below.

Directions For Each Student:

1. Color the flowers and butterfly.
2. Cut out the poem card and butterfly along the dotted lines.
3. Fold the poem card away from you on the solid line.
4. Cut the glue tab on the dotted lines.
5. Open the card.
6. Fold the card towards you, pushing the glue tab in as you fold.
7. Open the card so that the flowers stand upright.
8. Glue your butterfly cutout onto the glue tab.
9. Take your butterfly alphabet poem home and place it on a table for all to enjoy!

Name _____

All Aflutter With Poetry
Alphabet poem

Alphabet poetry is as easy as ABC!
Work with a partner.
Think about butterflies—how they look,
   what they do, what they eat.
Then write a butterfly word for each letter
   of the alphabet below.

B Is For Butterfly

Glue.   **Alphabet poetry**

A _____	J _____	S _____
B _____	K _____	T _____
C _____	L _____	U _____
D _____	M _____	V _____
E _____	N _____	W _____
F _____	O _____	X _____
G _____	P _____	Y _____
H _____	Q _____	Z _____
I _____	R _____	

All Aflutter With Poetry Unit

Materials Needed For Each Student:

handwriting paper
pencils
crayons or markers
scissors
hole punch (optional)
two-foot length of curling ribbon or yarn (optional)

How To Use Page 47

Give each student a white construction-paper copy of page 47. Discuss the format of haiku poetry by reading and working through the example at the top of the page together. Brainstorm with students a list of butterfly words. (Or have students refer to page 45, "B Is For Butterfly.") As a class, write a haiku poem to assure that students understand the process. Then have students complete their butterfly poems as directed on the reproducible. For added color, have students copy their poems with markers. Complete the butterfly projects as directed below. (Provide assistance as needed.) Invite students to read their poems aloud.

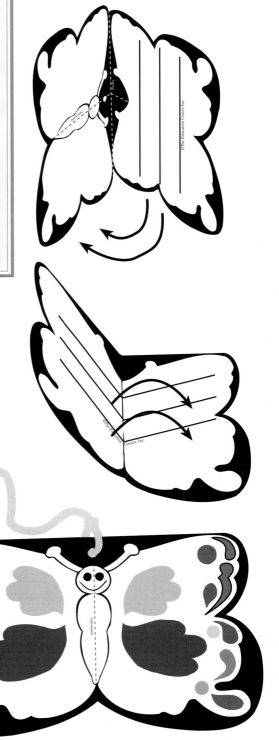

Directions For Each Student:

1. Cut the butterfly pattern out along the dark outline.
2. Fold the butterfly in half on the first dotted line.
3. Fold the butterfly in half again along the second dotted line.
4. Using a hole punch, punch a hole on the white dot at the top of the butterfly.
5. Tie a length of ribbon (or yarn) to the butterfly.

Suspend the students' butterfly projects from the ceiling for a bright display.

Variation

Have students complete steps 1–3 as directed above. Then have students present the butterfly cards to family or friends for a special pick-me-up.

High-Flying Haiku

A **haiku** is a three-line poem about nature.

Line **one** has **five syllables.** **(5)**
Line **two** has **seven syllables.** **(7)**
Line **three** has **five syllables.** **(5)**

Look at the haiku below.
Underline the syllables in each line.

A butterfly floats
through the summer air with ease,
a colorful sight.

On another sheet of paper, write a haiku about a butterfly.
Copy your haiku in your best handwriting on the lines of the butterfly below.
Color the other side of the butterfly.

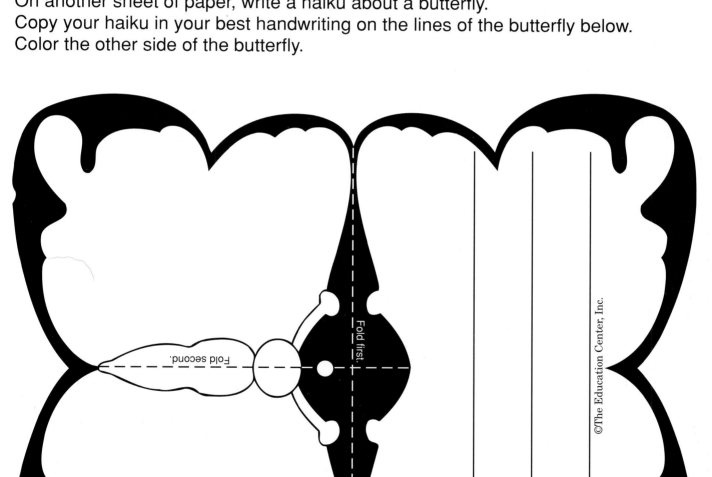

Name _____

Creative Couplets

A **couplet** is a two-line poem that rhymes:

   The butterfly's wings were so **bright**,
   They glimmered in the sun's **light!**

The lines of this poem end with words
   that rhyme (**bright, light**).

Read the following sentence.
Write the second line to create a couplet.
The last word of your sentence must rhyme
   with **white**.
Use the word box to help you.

The butterfly was orange and **white**,

_____ .

Word Box						
sight	fright	delight	might	tight	light	bite

Write a rhyming word for each word below.

   wing   fly   flutter   breeze

_____   _____   _____   _____

Choose one of the rhyming word pairs above.
Write a couplet using those words on the lines below.
Write the rhyming words in red.

_____

_____

Bonus Box: On the back of this sheet, write another couplet using one of the word pairs above.
Draw and color a picture to illustrate your couplet.

48